Glaciers

Precious McKenzie

ROURKE
PUBLISHING

www.rourkepublishing.com

www.rourkepublishing.com

PHOTO CREDITS: Title Page: © Emiecristea; Border: © jvdwolf; Page 4, 12: © Jason Register; Page 5: © Barsik; Page 6: © Nouk; Page 7: © Nolexa; Page 8: © igs942; Page 9: © Mmgrecu; Page 10: © Chillnz; Page 11: © Somatuscani; Page 12: © tabedin; Page 13: © herreid; Page 14: © Viktor Gmyria, © Kenneth Mellott; Page 15: © Michael Klenetsky; Page 16: © Peter Wollinga, © digital_eye; Page 17: © Kbrouwer; Page 18: © Granitepeaker; Page 19: © davelogon; Page 20: © wweagle; Page 21: © Yenwen Lu

Edited by Kelli L. Hicks

Cover Design by Nicola Stratford   bdpublishing.com
Interior Design by Renee Brady

Library of Congress Cataloging-in-Publication Data

McKenzie, Precious, 1975-
 Glaciers / Precious McKenzie.
   p. cm. -- (Eye to eye with endangered habitats)
 Includes bibliographical references and index.
 ISBN 978-1-61590-315-3 (Hard Cover) (alk. paper)
 ISBN 978-1-61590-554-6 (Soft Cover)
 1. Glaciers--Juvenile literature. I. Title.
 GB2403.8.M4 2011
 551.31'2--dc22
                    2010009269

Rourke Publishing
Printed in the United States of America, North Mankato, Minnesota
033010
033010LP

www.rourkepublishing.com - rourke@rourkepublishing.com
Post Office Box 643328 Vero Beach, Florida 32964

Table of Contents

River of Ice

Have you ever seen a frozen river? Now, imagine that frozen river covering a vast area, perhaps filling a mountain **valley**. Scientists call these icy formations glaciers.

Large amounts of snowfall and **frigid** temperatures encourage the formation of glaciers. It takes many, many years for glaciers to form.

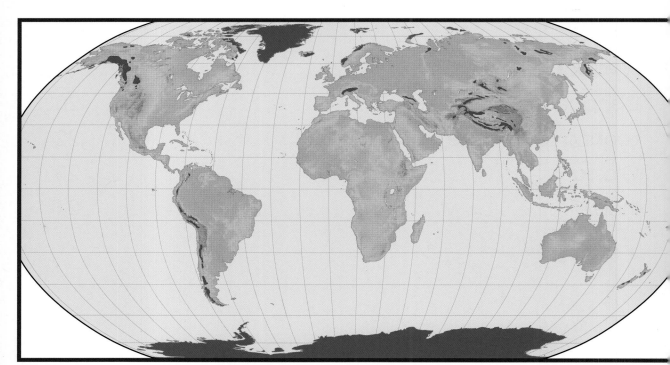

Glaciers cover almost ten percent of the Earth's surface.

People often think the climate of South America is warm and tropical. However, this glacier is found in Argentina. →

Glaciology

Glaciologists identified several types of glaciers. The two main types of glaciers are **continental** and valley glaciers.

Continental glaciers form in a dome shape and cover a large amount of land. Antarctica and Greenland have continental glaciers.

Sometimes continental glaciers are called ice sheets. If you ever travel to Greenland, you can see these ice sheets.

Located in the far north, near ➜ Canada, Greenland has the second largest ice body in the entire world!

The Force of Gravity

Valley glaciers begin to form at the top of mountains. Over time, **gravity** pulls the accumulated snow and ice down the mountain, into the valley.

The moving glacier looks like a river of ice. As the valley glacier travels, it churns up soil, rocks, and **sediment**. Because of the force of the movement, valley glaciers **erode**, or reshape, the natural landscape.

Many scientists, from all over the world, study the flow of valley glaciers so they can learn about the effects of climate change.

The Aletsch Glacier, Europe's largest glacier, → *stretches 66 miles (171 kilometers). It is 1 mile (1.6 kilometers) wide. Hikers have the chance to see marmots, lynx, and mountain sheep.*

On the Move

Glaciers can take hundreds or thousands of years to form. Some glaciers move slowly, creeping just a few feet over one hundred years. Others flow much faster, moving a few feet per month. Scientists call the fast moving glaciers surging glaciers.

People think the moving ice resembles a volcano's lava, only frozen!

Tourists love to visit the ➔
Briksdal Glacier in Norway.

The Tidewater

Can you guess which state in the United States has the most glaciers? The answer is Alaska. Alaska has more than 100,000 glaciers. Alaska is unique because it has a large number of tidewater glaciers. Rather than sliding into a valley, tidewater glaciers slide into the sea.

The United States government officially recognized Glacier Bay National Park in 1980.

Over 200 species of fish call these icy waters home. Marine mammals, such as Steller sea lions, humpback whales, and killer whales also live in these waters.

Visitors to Glacier Bay National Park can take sightseeing boat excursions to reach remote backcountry destinations.

Splash!

When large chunks of glaciers fall into the sea, scientists call these glacial pieces icebergs. Icebergs **calve** from under water as well, blasting massive pieces of ice up through the waves.

Just one-tenth of an iceberg floats above the water.

A calving glacier will destroy anything in its path.

Tourists love to see calving glaciers. Can ➜ you believe that people take boat rides just to see calving glaciers up close?

Norway

On land, glaciers create narrow gorges through mountains and coastlines. Norwegians call these **fjords**. People travel from all around the world to see Norway's impressive fjords.

At 127 miles long (205 kilometers), the Sognefjord in Norway is the second longest fjord in the entire world!

Some fjords in Norway are more than 4,265 feet (1,300 meters) deep and 124 miles (200 kilometers) long!

Visitors to the Geiranger fjord hike, canoe, raft, and take boat tours through the majestic gorges. →

A Valuable Resource

Every continent, except Australia, has glaciers. Glaciers provide water sources for rivers and lakes. People and animals depend on this water for survival.

The meltwater from the glaciers on Mount Everest provide fresh water for the people who live nearby in Nepal.

People in China use glacial → *water for their terraced farms.*

Disappearing Glaciers

Scientists think that rising global temperatures are causing glaciers to melt. According to their calculations, if the Earth's temperatures continue to rise, the glaciers in Montana's Glacier National Park will disappear by 2030.

Glaciers in the Andes and the Himalayas have already disappeared.

If you live in the continental United States, Glacier → National Park would be the closest place for you to travel to see the remaining glaciers.

Looking Toward the Future

Scientists all over the world are busy monitoring changes in glaciers. They track the annual size and movement of glaciers. Teams of scientists analyze **data** in order to learn more about **climate** change and its impact on glaciers.

Scientists are now encouraging people to reduce their use of **fossil fuels**, which will cut down carbon dioxide emissions, in order to slow global warming. You can help! Rather than drive a car everywhere, encourage your parents to walk or ride bicycles so we can preserve fossil fuels.

Scientists hope if we can prevent additional global warming, then we can preserve our majestic glaciers.

Glossary

calve (kav): to break off

climate (KLYE-mit): the weather in a part of the world

continental (KON-tuh-nuhnt-uhl): large area of land

data (DAY-tuh): information

erode (i-RODE): to wear away

fjords (FYORDZ): narrow inlets between cliffs

fossil fuels (FOSS-uhl FYOO-uhlz): oil, natural gases, or coal

frigid (FRIJ-id): very cold

glaciologists (GLAY-shee-OL-uh-gistz): people who study glaciers

gravity (GRAV-uh-tee): the force that pulls objects toward Earth

sediment (SED-uh-muhnt): rocks and dirt found at the bottom of a liquid, such as a river

valley (VAL-ee): low area between mountains

Index

Websites to Visit

www.nps.gov/glac/photosmultimedia/virtualtour.htm

www.sciencenewsforkids.org/articles/20080423/Feature1.asp

beyondpenguins.nsdl.org/

About the Author

Precious McKenzie was born in Ohio but has spent most of her life in south Florida. She has degrees in education and English from the University of South Florida. She currently lives in Florida where there are no glaciers.